Original title:
The Sea's Quiet Voice

Copyright © 2025 Creative Arts Management OÜ
All rights reserved.

Author: Giselle Montgomery
ISBN HARDBACK: 978-1-80587-270-2
ISBN PAPERBACK: 978-1-80587-740-0

Whispers Beneath the Waves

A crab with shades struts on the sand,
While fish gossip like they're in a band.
Jellyfish float, looking all divine,
Do they really care if they look fine?

Seaweed dances, a tangled delight,
Telling tales of full-moon nights.
Starfish giggle, stuck to a rock,
While dolphins parade with a tick-tock.

Murmurs of the Ocean Deep

Octopus winks with a playful grin,
Playing hide and seek with a fishy din.
Seahorses strut like they own the place,
While shrimp crack jokes at a snail's slow pace.

The waves chuckle as they lap at the shore,
As crabs hold court, oh what a score!
A clam jokes, 'I'm too shelled to care,'
And a flatfish sighs, 'I'm just too rare!'

Serenity in Salty Breezes

A pelican swoops down with style,
Making the fish jump just for a while.
Barnacles wear tiny hats of glee,
As the tide rolls in with a giggly spree.

The lighthouse winks, it has seen it all,
Whales telling jokes at the ocean ball.
Turtles giving high-fives in their slow, cool way,
While the sun sets brightly, ending the day.

Echoes of Distant Shores

Seagulls squawk like they own the breeze,
While sandcastles quiver, trying to please.
A rogue wave swipes at a beach bum's hat,
As crabs dance jigs, how about that?

Old shells gossip of love and strife,
While starfish debate the meaning of life.
With a flop and a wiggle, they scatter away,
Underneath the sun, where the sea creatures play.

Unspoken Dreams upon the Dune

A crab in a tux, he scuttles with grace,
Claiming the spotlight in this sandy place.
With a flip and a twirl, he steals the scene,
Dancing like no one knows what he means.

Seagulls gather 'round, casting sidelong glances,
As the crab takes a bow, it's a dance of chances.
His tiny shell sparkles, a real beach delight,
Under the sun's gaze, he dances in light.

Melodies Carried by the Wind

Whispers of waves, they tickle the shore,
A fish on a surfboard, asking for more.
It zips past a clam with a shocked sunny face,
'Catch me if you can!' — a slippery race.

The otters join in, with fishy chic style,
Waddling in rhythm, they make us all smile.
Round and round, they twirl, oh what a sight,
Nature's own band, performing at night.

Hidden Thoughts of the Briny Blue

Bubbles of laughter float up from below,
A dolphin pops up with a comedic show.
He wears a big hat, way too large for his head,
Spinning in circles, then off he sped.

The octopus laughs, with arms in a twist,
Playing hide and seek, he's too hard to miss.
With squid playing trumpet, it's quite the charade,
In the undersea theater, fun never fades.

The Canvas of Aquatic Dreams

In a world where the sand meets the ocean's embrace,
A starfish poses, it's all about grace.
With paint on his arms, he thinks he's Picasso,
Dabbing bright colors, what a wild fiasco!

Each wave carries tales where laughter takes flight,
Where seaweed performs in its disco delight.
A cartwheel by whales, a splashy ballet,
Underneath the moonlight, they clear out a way.

Caverns of Silence

In the depths where whispers play,
The fish all giggle, float away.
A crab tells jokes, a clownish sight,
As the octopus joins in, oh what a night!

The seaweed sways, a dancing crew,
With shells that laugh at the hullabaloo.
A starfish chuckles 'neath the waves,
Saying, 'We're just a bunch of knaves!'

Shards of Glass and Echoes

The waves bring stories, shiny and bright,
Sandcastles giggle with sheer delight.
A seagull squawks, 'Did you see that?'
While a jellyfish plays tag, imagine that!

Reflections shimmer, a comic show,
They whisper secrets only they know.
The dolphins leap, a splashing spree,
Making a splash—quite literally!

Lapping Hopes

Each wave a wish, with chuckles galore,
A plucky little crab, a sandcastle lore.
They laugh at tides that come rushing in,
While barnacles giggle, wearing a grin.

Seagulls swoop by, with jokes they deliver,
While sea cucumbers share their shiver.
Underwater humor, so salty and fine,
Tickling the fish who just want to dine.

The Weight of Water

With every push, the water does tease,
A wave winks at shore, 'Catch me, if you please!'
The rocks can't help but chuckle so loud,
While sea turtles glide, feeling so proud.

The ocean's a jester, with pearls to show,
Casting ripples like laughter below.
In this watery realm, all nonsense prevails,
As fish wish each other, 'Good luck with your tails!'

Rhythms of Reach

In the morning light, fish dance with glee,
A crab in a tux, doing the cha-cha, you see.
Waves tickle the shore, a foamy delight,
While seagulls squawk jokes, taking off in flight.

Barnacles gather, with tales to impart,
Of shipwrecked spaghetti and mermaids with art.
Starfish debate who is the best in the tide,
While shells gossip loudly, with sand as their guide.

Shadows of Shimmering Depths

The octopus plays hide and seek with a shoe,
A jellyfish jigs in a vibe that's askew.
Seaweed's a waltz, with a rhythm so swell,
While clam shells giggle, they're under a spell.

Coral formations, a city-like place,
Where fish try on frowns, but can't keep a face.
The tides tell tall tales with a flip and a roll,
As bubbles laugh softly, that's how they console.

Mystic Lull

In twilight's embrace, the dolphins all snicker,
While waves tell fairy tales, just a bit quicker.
Anemones sway, in a dance calm and bright,
As clowns of the reef laugh at their own sight.

The moon takes a peek, with a wink and a grin,
Making waves wave back as they swirl and spin.
A lighthouse beams softly, like an old friend's wink,
While fishes debate what color to think.

The Underbelly's Murmur

Beneath the blue waves, where the oddballs reside,
A sardine symposium, with humor to bide.
Crabs tell their tales, with claws held up high,
While an old flounder complains of the fry.

A seahorse stumbles, in a dance quite absurd,
And blubbers are chuckled, they're spread like a word.
The currents hum softly, a jolly old tune,
Swaying the ocean in the light of the moon.

The Lament of the Coral

Oh, I lost my best lipstick,
To a clam with a funny grin.
He wore it like a crown,
While I sulked in my shell.

The fish laughed all around,
As I tried to paint my face.
They said, 'You need a new look!'
But I just wanted my place.

A starfish took my socks,
Now my toes are feeling bare.
He claimed they were a fashion,
But I found it quite unfair.

So here I hum my blues,
With bubbles in the foam.
Who knew coral could be stylish?
In this watery home.

A Quiet Journey upon the Waves

Sailing on a rubber duck,
With a cat who thinks he's brave.
We drifted past old seaweed,
That looked like a mermaid's grave.

The jellyfish threw a party,
But forgot to send a note.
I showed up with dry snacks,
They were surprised at the boat.

A crab danced in the moonlight,
With moves that made me laugh.
I joined him for a waltz,
Though he stepped on my calf.

So across the ripples gliding,
We sang a silly tune.
Who knew that water travel,
Could lead to such monsoons?

Rippled Silences

In the hush where waves just giggle,
A dolphin cracks a joke.
Turtles ponder their next meal,
While a seagull steals my cloak.

Seaweed sways with laughter,
As a clownfish makes a face.
I tried to join the fun,
But tripped over a snail's place.

An octopus gave me pointers,
On how to blend in well.
But I laughed and waved too hard,
And splashed him with my shell.

In this quiet little cove,
Where craziness is the norm,
The sea speaks in whispers,
With a splash of humor warm.

Whispering Shells

In a shell, a secret lies,
Whispers soft like ocean sighs.
Crabs debate the latest news,
While fish laugh in painted hues.

Octopus with a sneaky wink,
Bubbles rise, and thoughts to think.
Starfish boast of sunny days,
As seaweed does a funky sway.

Veil of the Water's Edge

The tide rolls back with a silly grin,
Seagulls squawk about their kin.
Beach balls bounce, a playful scene,
While jellyfish float, quite serene.

Sandcastles topple, oh what a treat,
Pails and shovels all take a seat.
Laughter dances on the foamy crest,
As crabs tell tales of their latest quest.

Unwritten Verses of the Brine

A fish in shades of blue and green,
Recites a poem, not yet seen.
Gulls scribble lines in the sky,
While the seashells nod and sigh.

Hermit crabs dance a little jig,
In search of homes, each shell so big.
Waves play tag with the shore so bold,
Their stories in whispers, yet to be told.

Caress of the Still Tide

The waves hum softly, a quirky tune,
As fish prepare for a grand festoon.
Coral reefs with a giggle burst,
In underwater dances, they quench their thirst.

Sea cucumbers roll with flair,
While plankton twirl without a care.
The ocean laughs, its joy so bright,
In every splash, a happy sight.

Reflections on the Surface Still

When the water looks like glass,
Fish wear hats with a splash.
They gossip about the breeze,
And share secrets of the trees.

A seagull tries to take a dive,
But ends up in a spry jive.
Crabs clap hands with delight,
As the sun bids goodnight.

Jellyfish float, oh so lazy,
Waving like they're a bit crazy.
Starfish hold the best parties,
While octopuses go for smart martinis.

Each ripple holds a chuckle,
In this watery, wavy huddle.
If you listen close, take heed,
You'll hear laughter in the reeds.

Subtle Songs of the Seafoam

The frothy waves start to sing,
With humor, they twist and fling.
Shells have tales, they claim to share,
Of mermaids who comb their hair.

Sandy toes tap a beat,
While crabs groove in their seat.
Seagulls laugh at the fish's plight,
As they dive in for a bite.

Underneath, where bubbles rise,
Anemones tell silly lies.
Coral reefs do a little dance,
In an ocean full of chance.

Join the splash, don't be shy,
Let the water lift you high.
For in these waves, a whimsy swirls,
Where joy is found in salty pearls.

The Calm Between the Tides

In the calm, where winks abound,
The tide throws a curious sound.
Fishy flirts with subtle grace,
And bubbles plot their next embrace.

Wet towels wave as they dry,
A dolphin sneezes, a witty sigh.
Seashells chat about their day,
Dreaming of the ocean's play.

Each pebble wears a smiling face,
As they roll in a happy race.
Waves tickle sands with a tease,
Making joy in the salty breeze.

In this quiet, funny space,
Where laughter and water interlace.
Don't be stiff, join the fun,
It's a coastal laugh—two for one!

Gentle Refrains of the Coastal Breeze

The breeze whispers with a grin,
As kites begin to dance and spin.
Seagulls trade their sharp remarks,
While fishermen swap tall larks.

Drifting clouds play peek-a-boo,
Dropping rain, just a smooch or two.
Mermaids knit with seaweed threads,
Humor's tangled in their heads.

The crabs have formed a marching band,
Playing tunes on the golden sand.
Whales join in with a big bass line,
While dolphins leap, feeling divine.

So let's all hum along, my friend,
With the tide's laughter that won't end.
In this coastal melody so sweet,
Life's a dance, without missing a beat.

Quiet Rapture at Dusk

When the sun dips low, the waves all sigh,
A fish in a tuxedo swims on by.
Seagulls gossip, too, with such flair,
They mock the tourists without a care.

The crabs wear hats on their little heads,
Pinching each other, they prank like fools in beds.
A dolphin dances, does the twist,
While jellyfish ponder if they exist.

With laughter and splashes, the beach comes alive,
As sandcastles wobble, they just might survive.
Each sand grain a giggle, a playful tease,
Nature's own comedy, if you please!

At twilight's whisper, the night unfolds,
Mermaids giggle, sharing secrets untold.
The starfish chat, knitting tales of delight,
In this blissful waltz, all seems just right.

Tranquil Echoes of the Moonlit Sea

Beneath a blanket of shimmering light,
Wavelets form giggles that dance out of sight.
A crab plays the drum with great zeal,
While clams clap along, it's quite the deal!

Eels in bow ties slide past with a grin,
While turtles debate who should win the swim.
Jellyfish float by, fancying them bold,
Whispers of nonsense that never grow old.

The waves start to whisper, a corny joke,
As fish roll their eyes; they're a funny folk.
Stars twinkle brightly, joining in too,
Saying, "Well, this sea is a riot, who knew?"

With giggling surf and a sparkle of fun,
The night dances on 'til the rise of the sun.
As laughter and moonbeams swim hand in hand,
The ocean's a stage for the most whimsical band.

Ripple of the Unknown

Bubbles rise up with a curious pop,
Telling tall tales that never will stop.
A whale's on a phone, calling his mate,
Saying, "Come quick! You must see this fate!"

A crab shakes a leg, causing quite a scene,
Joined by a fish in a bright turquoise sheen.
"Dance party!" they squawk, with fins all a-flap,
While seaweed sways, a colorful chap.

A starfish claims he's a five-pointed king,
While barnacles laugh, "What a silly thing!"
The sea chuckles back, in ripples that play,
Joining in camaraderie all through the day.

With light-hearted jests and jokes from the deep,
The ocean keeps secrets that it loves to keep.
Adventures await with each twist and swirl,
In this laughable world, let joy unfurl!

Serenade of the Surf

The waves serenade with a silly tune,
Inviting each shell to come join the swoon.
A fish with a top hat leads the parade,
While otters surf on, unafraid to invade.

Seashells giggle as they tumble and roll,
Crabs wearing shades strike a pose, oh so droll.
With laughter and splashes, they dance in the foam,
Creating a ruckus that feels like home.

Mermaids gossip; they're witty, it seems,
Swapping wild stories of fantastical dreams.
The surf keeps on humming its joyful refrain,
As laughter swims wildly, like drops of the rain.

Each wave tells a secret, a twist of the fate,
A world full of mirth, where joy won't abate.
They giggle together, both near and afar,
In this jubilant place beneath the bright stars.

Celestial Harmony of the Ocean

A tide that dances, oh so spry,
Flipping fish and seagulls fly.
Jellybeans, the moon's delight,
Underwater laughter fills the night.

A crab with style in his old shell,
Waltzes with waves, could he tell?
Seashells gossip on the sand,
Whispers of a starfish band.

The starry sky joins in the fun,
With giggles from the setting sun.
Gull's gossip makes quite the scene,
What nonsense splashes in between!

Like bubbles bursting in a jest,
Each splash, a tale they bring the best.
The beach ball rolls with silly grace,
A sandy dance, a playful chase.

The Calm Behind the Storm

When tempests play and raindrops tick,
A fish performs a magic trick.
He swims in circles, dizzying spins,
While crabs prepare for ocean wins.

Thunder rumbles, but wait, what's this?
A dolphin leaps, as if to kiss.
With every crash and clumsy flail,
The ocean's giggle fills the sail.

Snails in shells, they slow it down,
While jellyfish wear crowns of brown.
In swirling waves, jokes twist and lurch,
As surfers ride their punchline perch.

But underneath, a secret cheer,
With each storm, the fish draw near.
They play charades, no fear, no harm,
In frothy tides, they find their charm.

Murmured Memories of the Nautilus

Deep in the ocean, tales unfold,
Of crusty gnomes and treasures old.
A nautilus hums a catchy tune,
While octopuses dance under the moon.

Seashells reminisce in a giddy chat,
About the time they all dressed a cat.
With pearls for eyes, they laugh and grin,
At silly stories of where they've been.

Fish sporting hats, they swim in style,
A parade of scales, each one a smile.
The jester turtle rolls on his back,
In a whirlpool of giggles and fishy quack.

A treasure map scribbled in ink,
Leads to a spot where fishies wink.
With lighthearted bounces, they all rejoice,
In whispers of laughter, they cheer and voice.

Nature's Forgotten Song

The whispering waves hum a tune,
In funky octaves beneath the moon.
A starfish strums on sandy shores,
While crabs applaud with clacking scores.

Seaspray sparkles, a flirty fling,
Teasing surfers to dance and swing.
In tangled kelp, the giggles rise,
As turtles trade their sassy lies.

Bubbles bounce, it's quite the show,
With a seaweed twist and a splashy row.
Every current holds a jest,
Nature's laugh, oh what a fest!

A fish in shades, who knew he'd pose?
In the grand sea stage, the laughter flows.
In the quiet, fun's not far,
For all know well, waves are bizarre!

Solitude of the Salted Wind

The wind whispers secrets, oh what a tease,
With salt on my lips, it knows how to squeeze.
I chase after whispers, they giggle and flee,
Making me trip on my own two left feet.

A seagull calls over, with sass in the air,
He plucks at my sandwich, does he even care?
With crumbs on my shirt and a wink from the sun,
I laugh at my fate as I finally run.

The waves clap their hands, splash water with might,
While I juggle sea shells, a comical sight.
Balancing laughter on a tip of a wave,
Oh, how I wish to be a humorist brave!

The breeze starts to chuckle, sways palm trees around,
Kicking up sand, leaving giggles unbound.
With each silly tumble, I roll on the floor,
This solitude's funny; I crave for some more!

Solitary Sirens

Down by the shore, where mermaids might sing,
A pastry shop lost in a shellfish fling.
They lure folks with laughter, a pastry parade,
Seducing the gullible, oh what a charade!

A siren in stripes, selling taffy with flair,
Lures sailors with double, to savor the air.
They sing sweet enchantments, a song crafted bright,
While I sit here munching on fudge under moonlight.

With flippers and giggles, they dance 'round the bay,
Claiming each jellyfish has something to say.
They coax me to join in their silly ballet,
But I trip on my feet; oh, how they convey!

So here I remain, where the salty winds swirl,
In this bounty of humor, my heart starts to twirl.
These sirens of joy, in their seaweed disguise,
Leave you laughing for hours, oh what a surprise!

The Hushed Call of the Coast

In twilight's embrace, a soft chuckle begins,
As crabs hold a meeting, plotting their sins.
The rocks shoot their wisecracks, the shells join the fun,
With seaweed-topped ties, they dance just like one.

Beneath starry skies, they're planning a feast,
Where plankton wears glasses and dances the least.
The wind bursts with laughter, tickling my ear,
Oh, the coast's hushed calling makes humor so clear!

While waves roll in gently, they tease with a splash,
As clams wink with mischief, and gulls start to dash.
The night winds conspire to coax out my grin,
With such jests in the air, who needs to fit in?

Alone on this beach, where the laughter does bloom,
I take in the quiet, feel joy in the room.
With crustacean pals, and the stars shining bright,
I find it's a comedy to end every night!

Beneath the Stars and Waves

Under stars that wink, and moonbeams that play,
I found a lost flounder who giggled all day.
He told me such tales of the fish in disguise,
In bubbles and swirls, they'd send laughs to the skies.

A starfish in shades, lounging smooth on a rock,
Practices his stand-up with seabird's tick-tock.
With an audience square of ocean and foam,
He splashily jokes of how crab lost his comb!

From jellyfish jests to the dolphin's great skill,
Every corner of ocean adds spark to the thrill.
I chuckle in comfort, my worries all tossed,
In this watery world, I've truly not lost!

So let the waves sing, let the tides spin the yarn,
For 'neath the night's star, fresh laughter is born.
With friends in the depths, and joy on the rise,
Each ripple of humor ignites the night skies!

When Waves Remember

Waves giggle as they crash,
Splashing about in frothy glee.
They hold sand dollars like treasure,
Whispering tales of jellyfish free.

Seagulls squawk in a comical flight,
Dancing on breezes, oh what a sight!
Fishes flip in hilarious haste,
Waving goodbye, never a waste.

Shells collect stories, some fishy indeed,
One wore sunglasses, a surfer's creed.
They chat with the pebbles, quite out of tune,
In the sunlit expanse, life's a cartoon.

So when you stroll by, hear their cheer,
They crack up like comics, loud and clear.
For laughter's the spark in the salty air,
Reminding us all, enjoy and share!

Ferns of Forgotten Dreams

Ferns sway softly, no rhythm in sight,
But watch closely, they're ready for flight.
They flail their fronds like they're in a race,
Tickling the breezes, keeping up pace.

Once they whispered a secret so sly,
'Twas about mermaids, oh my, oh my!
With hair made of kelp and a grace that astounds,
They teach the ferns intricate dance rounds.

Each fern's a dreamer, lost on the shore,
Hoping to glide, but they trip on the floor.
One shouted, "Hey! I'm the King of the Pond!"
While another just giggled, "That's quite a blonde!"

So gather around, let's hear them in chat,
Their leafy ambitions, covered in spat.
Ferns of forgotten dreams laugh in delight,
In this quirky tale of nature's own light.

Silent Horizons

The horizon stares, a twitch in its gaze,
Teasing the sky in a mystical haze.
Clouds wear a frown, oh what a display,
As if they forgot what they wanted to say.

Paddling on boats, thoughts drift away,
Rowing in circles, what a silly ballet!
Mermaids in chorus, each line a delight,
Join in the giggles from morning to night.

Fish chat about fashion, fins all a-flare,
"Is this tail in or out? Do we even care?"
In the distance, a whale makes a bid,
"Sorry, my friends, I'm just trying to hid!"

So gaze at the horizon, let laughter abound,
For in silence, a merry chorus is found.
The wonders of oceans, the humor out there,
Bring joy from the depths, feel free to share!

A Tide's Contemplation

The tide rolls in with a curious grin,
It ponders the rocks, who wears the best skin?
Barnacles boast, "We're tough as can be!"
While tides just chuckle, "You've stuck to debris!"

In a game of tic-tac-toe on the sand,
Waves laugh, "Oh friend, you really can't stand!"
With each gentle lapping, a splashy retort,
As shells gather 'round for a seaside sport.

Seagulls circle like kids on a swing,
Flinging down snacks that the crabs start to bring.
The shoreline's a playground of antics galore,
Where nature's your friend, and the fun's never poor.

So join in the jest of this watery scene,
Dance with the tide as it floats in between.
Take joy from the banter and peaceful delight,
For laughter and currents keep spirits so bright!

Harmony of the Morning Tide

Waves rolling in with a giggle so loud,
They splash at the shore, drawing a crowd.
Seabirds make jokes, in their awkward flight,
Cracking the shells, what a silly sight!

Sandcastles wobble, as kids build with glee,
A tower that looks like a lopsided tree.
Kids run and trip, in a sand-filled race,
While crabs wave their claws, making a fuss of their space!

Shadows Cast by Gentle Waves

Waves dance along, casting shadows on sand,
A crab wriggles by, waving his hand.
The sun winks down, as seagulls take flight,
They squawk out jokes, what a comical sight!

The seaweed wiggles, like a creature in play,
As fish swim by, in their stealthy ballet.
Everyone's laughing, it's a riot of cheer,
In the shadows of waves, there's nothing to fear!

Whispers of the Tides

The tide tips its hat, with a splash and a grin,
It sways back and forth, it's a whimsical spin.
Shells hoot with laughter as they roll on the beach,
While dolphins play tag, giving each other a screech!

The tides whisper secrets, in bubble-filled prose,
As the odd starfish sings, with a very strange pose.
The ocean just chuckles, as it swirls around,
With its funny little ripples, it makes quite a sound!

Songs Beneath the Waves

Coral reefs giggle, with colors so bright,
Fish line up neatly, for a chorus tonight.
Octopuses juggle, in a watery show,
While sea turtles sway, taking it slow!

Bubbles rise high, like balloons in the air,
Each one a tune, floating without a care.
With seaweed as percussion, they jam and they play,
Underwater antics, in a comical way!

Conversations with Distant Horizons

The fish in suits discuss today,
They strive to find a proper way.
A crab critiques the ocean's flow,
While dolphins giggle, putting on a show.

The waves are laughing, what a treat,
As sea turtles dance on dainty feet.
A starfish jokes, all arms extended,
In this bizarre chat, they're all pretended.

Seagulls squawk their nonsense tales,
While barnacles are trading sails.
They debate the best pizza crust,
While jellyfish float and lose their trust.

With shells as phones, they dial the sky,
Calling up the clouds, "Oh, why so shy?"
The breezes carry their laughter far,
As they share secrets with the evening star.

Solitudes of the Ocean Floor

Deep down below where few will tread,
The shrimp and squid have just been fed.
An octopus writes in ink so blue,
A deep-sea novel none will view.

A fish who's shy has lost his way,
As clams compose a jazz ballet.
The bubbles rise with stories bold,
Of treasure chests that rarely sold.

A turtle, wise, dispenses tips,
While anglerfish play wacky quips.
They shake their fins, they wiggle tails,
In this odd realm, laughter prevails.

They play rock-paper-scissors with a shell,
Each time it's lost, they laugh and yell.
Though solitude reigns far from the light,
They find their fun in the depths of night.

Reveries in the Gulf's Embrace

In the Gulf's hug, where silliness grows,
Barracudas twist into funny bows.
Conch shells gossip about the tide,
As prancing seahorses take a ride.

Anemones wave like they're in a band,
While playful otters prank all the sand.
The pelicans drop their catch and laugh,
As fish swim past, escaping the chaff.

Seaweed sways, it joins the groove,
While clowns dive down with a silly move.
With a flip and a flap, they break from norms,
In this dreamy place where laughter storms.

They throw a party with shells all around,
As crabs play drums, making a sound.
In this embrace where antics breathe,
The Gulf holds joys, it never leaves.

Soft Whispers at Dusk

At dusk, the waves begin to giggle,
As light plays tricks, waves start to wiggle.
A clam cracks jokes while fish roll their eyes,
Under the twilight's colorful skies.

Starfish tell tales of their night-time strolls,
While seagulls compete in playful brawls.
The lighthouse winks, a cheeky twinkle,
As silence breaks with laughter's crinkle.

A little crab scuttles, chasing the glow,
With every quick step, it's quite the show.
"Why cross the sand?" asks a wise old frog,
"Just float with ease on this midnight fog."

In these soft whispers, the day takes flight,
Creatures unite in the golden light.
As dusk wraps the ocean in blissful tones,
Laughter echoes in hushed undertones.

Embracing Stillness by the Dock

A crab in pajamas strolls the pier,
Planning his dinner, oh dear, oh dear!
Seagulls are laughing, with chips in their beak,
While fish tell jokes that only they speak.

Eels in tuxedos swim with such grace,
Waving to turtles in a slow-motion race.
The dock creaks and groans as if it's alive,
Wondering if crabs can really thrive.

A fisherman snores in the boat, so secure,
Dreaming of mermaids, but none are pure.
With laughter and splashes, the sunset begins,
Around comes the breeze, and oh, how it grins!

The stars start to giggle; the moon winks in glee,
As bubbles rise up from the depths of the sea.
No need for a lifeguard or anyone bold,
Just a fish with a story and some laughter to hold.

The Language of Drifting Clouds

Fluffy sheep roam in skies up so high,
Muttering secrets—oh me, oh my!
A whale in the distance gives a loud cheer,
Wonders what clouds taste like, with a heart full of beer.

Each puff whispers tales of great ocean quests,
Telling of turtles that wear tiny vests.
A dolphin plays tag, a real clown of the deep,
While jellyfish giggle and lose track of sleep.

The breeze throws confetti, it's a party for free,
As the sun pokes its head, looking for tea.
Every wave chuckles, a jubilant dance,
While sandcastles giggle in a sandy romance.

But as daylight fades, the clouds ruffle their hair,
Planning next week's gossip, a real hoot, I swear.
What nonsense awaits in the twilight's embrace?
Just wait till the stars join this cosmic race!

Calm Reflections of a Setting Sun

The sun wears a hat, quite stylish and round,
Casting blush on the waves, a big splashy sound.
Fish turn their backs, pretending to be shy,
But they can't resist a show, oh my, oh my!

A starfish winks, with a twinkle and grin,
Sharing tall tales of where he's been.
The tide tickles toes, on sand that's so warm,
Creating a laughter, a playful charm.

Crabs juggle shells in the glow of the dusk,
Finding this whole scene just too much to husk.
With every dipped splash, there's a giggle and cheer,
And the ocean collects every single weird tear.

As evening descends with a colorful fling,
The moon steps in, ready to sing.
And all through the night, while the sea gently hums,
Comes the music of tides, where the laughter just thrums.

Lyrics of the Deep Blue Unknown

Bubbles rise up with a soft little pop,
Disco fish shimmy, they'll never stop.
Seahorses tango while clams keep the beat,
Shells snap their fingers, oh, they're feeling so neat.

The octopus conducts with eight little arms,
While his jellyfish friends give the crowd all their charms.

A starfish, stage fright? Nope, not tonight,
He struts down the aisle, what a flashy sight!

Waves chatter gossip, while the sun spins its tale,
Of mermaids and dolphins who never will fail.
With laughter echoing under the deep, dark sky,
The salty serenade makes even fish cry.

As night falls in rhythm, the deep starts to sway,
Every creature smiling, what a merry display!
Down in the blue, where the sea's got the groove,
Nothing is dull when you find your own move.

Embrace of the Quiet Waters

Bubbles rise and fish make faces,
The tide competes in friendly races.
Seagulls squawk, but what's their deal?
A clam just sighed—'Oh, what a meal!'

Waves lapped back with gentle giggles,
As starfish jived with wiggly wiggles.
Crabs found shade and sipped on tea,
An octopus just winked at me!

Drifting boats like cozy beds,
With sleepy sails and snuggly threads.
A dolphin danced, made quite a splash,
Then tripped on plankton, what a crash!

Oysters snickered, pearls in tow,
While jellyfish put on a show.
The ocean chuckled, soft and clear,
Whispering secrets for those who hear.

Subtle Rhythms of the Shore

Sandcastles rise with lofty dreams,
While waves conspire in playful schemes.
A beach ball bounces, that's no fluke,
It's hard to catch, just like a book!

Flip-flops stumble, kids run wild,
An ice cream truck, oh, what a child!
Sunscreen slips like a sly old fox,
While seagulls steal our last two socks!

Tanning lotion, oh what a smell,
It mixes well with a seashell's yell.
A crab in shades struts down the line,
Thinking he's classy, looking divine!

Shells whisper tales of what they've seen,
While a mermaid laughs and takes a glean.
The tide ticks like a timeless clock,
Making beachcombers do the rock!

Silenced by the Horizon

The sun hangs low, a golden eye,
As seaweed wiggles, saying hi!
Mermaids gossip in swirls of foam,
While puzzled fish think they're at home.

Waves carry laughter, soft and light,
A pelican dreams of taking flight.
A crab with shades takes a stroll,
While snails wear shells as funny bowls!

The horizon stretches, what a tease,
It's hard to tell where it meets the breeze.
Shy little waves try to act bold,
But trip over shells—how very old!

Saltwater tickles and makes you smile,
As laughter drifts for quite a while.
The breeze hums tunes, kindly and sly,
While turtles watch with a thoughtful eye!

Reflections in Liquid Calm

Mirrors shimmer with tales untold,
Fish play poker, taking bold.
The water's still, like a fairy's dream,
Where frogs practice their singing team.

Stars wink down from their evening stage,
While crabs recite from the gossip page.
Flamingos strike a cooking pose,
While turtles debate their next big clothes!

Ripples dance like happy feet,
As jellybeans float, oh what a treat!
The calmness giggles, twinkles bright,
Making shadows that dance at night.

Whispers travel through the light,
As shells share tales of their brave flight.
In the hush, mischief's alive,
For every wave seeks to jive!

Echoes of the Deep

Bubbles bubble, fish all prance,
Starfish wiggle, in a dance.
Crabs are scuttling, what a sight,
Underwater, they shout with delight.

Waves are giggling, seaweed sways,
Octopuses play in funny ways.
Turtles grin with shells so bright,
Splashing around, oh what a night!

Mollusks laughing, shells in tow,
Jellyfish with a glowing glow.
Barnacles chat, oh what a fuss,
In a clam-shell, they make a bus!

A dolphin's joke echoes so clear,
While fishy friends hold back a cheer.
With every splash, the sea grows wise,
In bubbles of laughter, joy will rise.

Murmurs of Ocean Dreams

Clams are gossiping, soft and slow,
Whale songs bubble, high and low.
The sand dollars giggle, all in a heap,
While the shy sea cucumbers start to peep.

Seahorses sway, dressed to impress,
While sea otters play, nothing but mess.
Fish in bowties swim by so proud,
Making a splash, they gather a crowd.

Eels in bright hues dance to a tune,
While snoozing seals sleep under the moon.
Each ripple carries a chuckle aboard,
As the ocean's humor can't be ignored.

Starfish flip with a wink and a grin,
Whispering secrets of mischief within.
The tides keep rolling, laughter like foam,
Together they sing, a watery home.

Beneath the Surface Still

Mermaids chuckle, stealing the show,
With fins that sparkle, they surely glow.
Bubbles pop with a giggly sound,
As friends in shells gather around.

The ocean floor, a stage so bright,
Featuring fish in a quirky light.
Crabs with crowns preside with flair,
While sea turtles grow big hair!

Lanternfish sparkle, a disco ball,
Throwing a party, inviting all.
Corals giggle in weathered hues,
As they sway to the ocean's blues.

A whale blows bubbles, humor afloat,
With each jolly splash, they happily gloat.
The ocean's depths are filled with glee,
Where creatures dance, wild and free.

Lullabies from the Abyss

Dolphins chirp in a sandcastle tune,
Seashells echo under the moon.
Anemones sway, tickling the sand,
While sea slugs hold hands, feeling grand.

Mermen juggle bright silver fish,
While sea lions applaud with a swish.
The gentle waves, a playful hum,
As creatures below begin to drum.

Pufferfish puff up, creating a fuss,
Waving their fins, making a bus.
With jellyfish gliding like they own the night,
The whole sea giggles, what a sight!

As lullabies ripple through shimmering blue,
The ocean whispers her playful brew.
With every wave, laughter will rise,
In the watery depths, joy never hides.

Tranquil Currents of Thought

When waves burp softly, I just chuckle,
It's nature's way of sharing a tuckle.
Seagulls gossip high in the bluest skies,
While crabs do a dance, don their best ties.

Jellyfish float like balloons on a spree,
Wondering where their next dance party will be.
Starfish lounge, like they're on a cruise,
As barnacles play peekaboo with the blues.

Fish dart around, all glimmer and flash,
Guess they think they're stars, oh what a bash!
The ocean giggles with every small rip,
Weighing the humor behind each quip.

So next time you hear a splash or a giggle,
Know that beneath, the waves do a wiggle.
With every bubble, a joke takes flight,
In salty depths, humor's pure delight.

Secrets Held in Tidal Silences

In quiet depths, the whispers get silly,
An octopus jokes, with arms oh so frilly.
Mussels gossip about clams on the sand,
While starry skies wink at a fishy band.

Tide pools bubble like pots on a stove,
Where crabs put on acts, in their own little grove.
Seashells listen, with ears open wide,
Collecting tall tales from the watery tide.

Octopuses peek from their hidden retreats,
Throwing ink blots, like perplexing beats.
Each splash is a snicker, each ripple a grin,
In a world of wonders where laughter creeps in.

So if you stroll where the waterlines play,
Listen closely; nature's cracking a fray.
With every ebb, a chuckle does swell,
In muted secrets, all's well—can't you tell?

Harmony of the Undercurrents

Below the surface, the fish strike a pose,
As seaweed sways to the rhythm it knows.
Crabs play the drums on their rocky abode,
With bubbles afloat, they rock the code.

Schools of fish swim in coordinated lines,
Making a conga from the snags and the pines.
They laugh at the dolphins, all slick and spry,
As they flip and they flounder, oh my, oh my!

Anemones brush their flowing hair with pride,
While barnacles gossip, making waves side to side.
The ocean's an orchestra, kooky and bright,
With each gentle ripple, they create pure delight.

So next time you gaze at the waters so deep,
Know that cheeky fish are awake, not asleep.
Their laughter echoes like bubbles set free,
In undulating antics, they dance with glee.

Lullabies of the Moonlit Waters

Under the moon, the waves start to giggle,
As sleep-deprived crabs try to do a jiggle.
Seahorses snicker while twirling around,
In shimmering dreams, they're lost and found.

The starry night holds secrets in its grasp,
While fishes debate, sharing jokes in a clasp.
The tide gently hums a lullaby tune,
That tickles the surface and brightens the dune.

So a whale may snore with a splashing sound,
While dolphins dive deep, joyfully unbound.
The night is alive with a symphony sweet,
A whimsical ballet that pulls at your feet.

So close your eyes to the water's soft sway,
Full of jests and whispers that play through the day.
In the calm light, where the moon shines a way,
Laughter ripples softly; it's here to stay.

Gentle Currents of Thought

Fish wearing hats swim with glee,
A crab's doing salsa near a tree.
The lighthouse stands tall, with a watchful eye,
While seagulls gossip as they fly.

A turtle snoozes, dreaming of races,
While octopuses practice their funny faces.
The jellyfish jive, in a dance so bold,
Whispering secrets that never get old.

Sandcastles titter at waves that approach,
"Is that the tide?" asks a curious roach.
The shells on the beach crack jokes so fine,
While sunlight glistens like bubbly wine.

As snails deliver news that's absurd,
The starfish laugh, not saying a word.
So join in the fun as we splash and sway,
With laughter that echoes the whole summer day.

Secrets of the Briny Blue

Why did the clam refuse to share?
It had a secret that was quite rare.
A dolphin told jokes with a cheeky grin,
While waves rolled by, like they were in on the spin.

A crab in a tux, thinking he's sly,
Tries to impress a fish swimming by.
The seaweed dances, swaying to tunes,
While anchors drop down, confusing the loons.

The barnacles whisper beneath the waves,
"Why are we stuck? Let's misbehave!"
A whale plays tag with a big ol' ship,
While mermaids giggle, giving a flip.

As the sun dips low, painting the scene,
Fish start karaoke, all dressed in green.
So listen closely, take a wild guess,
The ocean's just silly, and loving the mess.

The Ocean's Soft Serenade

The sea sings sweetly, a tune so light,
With frogs on the shore croaking in delight.
A dolphin attempts a high-flying dive,
With a splash so big, it gives fish a jive!

Waves tickle toes as they run away,
Seagulls swoop down, yelling, "Hey, hey!"
The tide knows the rhythm, the flotsam hums,
A chorus of laughter from the fins and gums.

Starfish play tag on the ocean floor,
While eels joke about their tangled lore.
A whale cracks a joke about his size,
While turtles roll over, laughing with cries.

So gather your friends for a dance by the shore,
As the ocean serenades forevermore.
It's a giggle buffet, and everyone's sweet,
Join in the fun; let life feel the beat!

Tranquil Depths

In tranquil depths, the fish hold a ball,
With seaweed snacks, they dance and enthrall.
Octopuses twist in a fashion so grand,
While a shrimp gives a speech, trying to stand.

A coral reef shines, hosting a feast,
Where clowns share the stage, laughter released.
The kraken tells tales, with a wink and a smile,
Making waves with his stories that stretch every mile.

Bubbles pop up, like giggles afloat,
While turtles wear ties, trying to gloat.
The gulls on the rocks are a riotous crew,
Making jokes about waters so deep and so blue.

As twilight descends, the stars start to wink,
The sea's soft giggles make us all think.
There's joy in the tides, a melody bright,
In tranquil depths where all feels just right.

A Palette of Blue Whispers

Waves slap the shore, making a fuss,
Seagulls squawk, Uncle Lou's on the bus.
The sand tickles toes, a grainy surprise,
While fish giggle loudly at the catch of the eyes.

Crabs wear their armor, in a dance quite absurd,
Chasing each other, not saying a word.
The sun plays with shadows on a vibrant quilt,
As jellyfish jiggle with minimal guilt.

Tides have their secrets, they bubble with glee,
As shells tell tall tales, oh, who can foresee?
Mariners laugh from their boats on the rise,
Trading their stories like fishy old pies.

A hat on a wave gives a nod and a wink,
While octopuses ponder, just staring and think.
Life in the brine isn't always so sane,
With todos of bubbles and giggles for gain.

Timeless Stillness of the Harbor

Ducks in a row, with their boats in a line,
Playing cards on the dock, sipping brine-infused wine.
A fisherman yawns, his tackle all tangled,
While deep in thought, his sandwiches dangled.

The lighthouse is grinning, a permanent smile,
Waving to seagulls who float with such style.
The benches complain of the weight they must bear,
As fishermen gossip of adventures rare.

A buoy hums softly, a lullaby sweet,
While crabs play hopscotch on some fishermen's feet.
The tide rolls in, with a comedic flair,
As dolphins suggest that they dance in midair.

Old masts creak like knees at a dance hall so bright,
As stars come to join, dancing all through the night.
With laughter and splashes, the harbor's alive,
In this quirky ballet, everyone thrives.

Shadows Underneath the Surf

At dusk, the shadows take on silly forms,
Mermaids trade tales of their most epic storms.
Shark swims by wearing a mustache that spins,
As clownfish giggle, just waiting to win.

Seashells whisper secrets from under the tide,
While sunken ships chuckle, not trying to hide.
The surf gets ticklish, with each playful wave,
While crabs in tuxedos practice how to behave.

Anemones bounce like they just learned to dance,
While starfish contemplate their next ocean romance.
The kelp fields sway like a band full of cheer,
Giving a wave when another wave's near.

Bubbles rise up; they just can't contain,
A dolphin's snickers cause ripples of pain.
Laughter abounds as all creatures unite,
In this underwater circus, a whimsical sight.

The Ocean's Unseen Canvas

The wind draws pictures upon the blue skies,
While fish put on hats, preparing to prize.
Starfish play artists, with paint from the floor,
Leaving handprints of ink, what a colorful score!

Seagulls, like critics, swoop down to inspect,
Giving their ratings with honks to affect.
Whales hum a tune, a melody bright,
As shells on the shore throw a party tonight.

A crab with a beret directs the parade,
While jellyfish twirl in a frothy charade.
With laughter exploding like bubbles in sun,
Everyone's painting, each stroke is pure fun.

So listen closely, the brush strokes are near,
Whispering tales of the ocean so clear.
In this magical world, with giggles so grand,
Each wave tells a story, like art in the sand.

Reflections from the Abyss

Waves whisper secrets, a fish wears a tie,
A crab with a monocle, oh my, oh my!
Jellyfish dance, in a wobbly swirl,
A seashell sings, a marine world whirl.

Mermaids giggle, tickled by foam,
While dolphins throw parties, far from their home.
A starfish plays poker, with shells on its hand,
The tide rolls in, like a comedic band.

Old seagulls gossip, with feathers askew,
While barnacles argue, on what's latest in blue.
They say the sand knows all the best jokes,
Blowing laughter, it tickles the folks.

So listen closely, to the waters that sway,
For laughter's a tide that will brighten your day.
The depths keep their humor, both silly and sly,
In the heart of the ocean, where giggles can fly.

Lingering Traces on the Shore

Footprints in sand, a crab takes a stroll,
While flip-flops are hiding, in a deep, dark hole.
Seagulls debating, over last night's fry,
A clam brings a story, how time seems to fly.

Sponges wear hats, in the warm summer sun,
An octopus juggles, oh, what a fun run!
Seashells play marbles, rolling with glee,
As seaweed joins in, in a jubilee spree.

A beach ball gets stolen, by the tide's sneaky hand,
Kites in the wind, dancing over the sand.
The waves laugh and tumble, as a surfboard swoops,
Creating a splash, with giggles in groups.

As sun sets to sleep, and the stars shine so bright,
The ocean still chuckles, into the night.
For on shores of laughter, where silliness blends,
The joy of the water, just never ends.

Calmed by the Moon's Gaze

The moon grins wide, with a twinkle and shine,
As fish tell tall tales, sipping seaweed wine.
Turtles in tuxedos, dance on the rocks,
While sea cucumbers gossip, with lots of shock.

A dolphin, so dapper, in his fancy attire,
Stands ready to surf, on an old driftwood lyre.
The starry sky winks, at the whale's wise song,
While fish play the trumpet, it's a party, not long.

Glow-in-the-dark plankton, takes center stage,
As sardines perform, flipping page after page.
They throw confetti, made of tiny shells,
As the breeze carries laughter, like oceanic bells.

So under the moon, as the waters chuckle,
The night finds its rhythm, in a playful shuffle.
For in this vast space, where the funny tides roam,
The laughter is endless, forever a home.

Waters Unseen

In depths where the jellyfish play hide and seek,
A shrimp turns philosopher, oh, don't be meek!
The bubbles are secrets, escaping with glee,
As sea foam tells tales, of what might just be.

Squids use their ink, for a rainbow of art,
While clownfish offer the best tip-off for part.
Watch out for that wave, it's a slippery prank,
That sends snorkelers tumbling, right into the tank.

Coral reefs giggle, in luminescent glow,
And anemones wiggle, in seas that they know.
With each gentle ripple, life's banter unfurls,
Such laughter and joy, in this underwater world.

So dive into the depths, where shenanigans brew,
And listen closely, for a joke or two.
The waters, though hidden, have stories to tell,
With laughter to share, in their magical shell.

Echoing Footprints in Sand

Waves tease the shore with playful glee,
Each step I take, a giggle's decree.
Seagulls caw like they run the show,
But who's the real star? The sand below!

Footprints vanish with a quick retreat,
As if the sand plays hide and seek.
I laugh as I trip, then tumble so grand,
While shells whisper secrets, all unplanned.

Dancing barefoot, I feel the heat,
A crab joins the fun; oh what a feat!
He scuttles away with a side-eyed glance,
In the rhythm of waves, we all prance!

So here I stand, a joyful mess,
With each wild wave, I feel so blessed.
The ocean's got jokes, it seems quite clear,
With every splash, it brings out my cheer!

The Soundless Song of Storms Past

Once there was thunder, fierce and bold,
A song of mischief, if truth be told.
Rain danced on rooftops, tickled the trees,
Made umbrellas turn into boats on the breeze!

Clouds rolled in, all grumpy and gray,
Yet even they humorously play.
Lightning chuckled, flashing a grin,
While the wind swirled laughing, causing a spin.

Puddles became pools, a splashy affair,
As ducks waddled in, without a care.
Each step through the muck, a ballet of sorts,
Held together by laughter, like comedy shorts.

When storms passed by, I wiped my face,
And the sun returned with a teasing embrace.
Nature knows fun, it's clear from the past,
A symphony of giggles, oh so vast!

Beneath the Silence, Life

Bubbles rise like popcorn, all aglow,
Beneath the calm, there's a party below.
Jellyfish jiggle, in their transparent suits,
While starfish chuckle in their funky boots.

Coral reefs hum with a busy refrain,
Fish together dance, a joyful domain.
Lobsters drag race through the vibrant expanse,
While seaweed sways, putting on a dance!

A whale breaks surface with a giggly splash,
Sending sprays of water in an exuberant dash.
Turtles slow-waddle, a sight to behold,
In a world that's silent, with laughter bold.

So under the waves, don't think it's all calm,
There's a hidden carnival, full of charm.
Life bubbles forth, with chuckles and cheer,
In the depths of the ocean, where silliness steers!

Hush of the Ocean Floor

Under the waves, where stillness is king,
There's a giggling clam, doing its thing.
Seabed tickles from curious fish,
Reviving old tales, what a fine dish!

A flounder flat-jumps, trying to hide,
In the blanket of sand, what a funny ride!
Starfish take selfies, with shells all around,
Each click of the lens, a whole new sound.

Octopuses sport hats, looking so cool,
In this silent kingdom, they rule the school.
With each silent wave, secrets will swirl,
Where laughter is hidden in the ocean's pearl.

So hush now, dear friend, listen close and hear,
The whispers of mischief that drift ever near.
Beneath the calm surface, fun does abound,
In the hush of the ocean, joy can be found!

Veiled Whispers Beneath the Waves

Fish gossip softly, like sailors at play,
Jellyfish giggle, in a wobbly way.
Crabs in tuxedos, try hard to impress,
While sea cucumbers just wear their distress.

Whales tell tales of the days gone by,
Of sunken ships and a rubber duck's cry.
Octopi painting with creativity's flair,
While a starfish just sits, with a blank stare.

Seagulls complain of the fish slow to bite,
They squawk about sandwiches, what a true plight!
Mermaids are laughing, their hair filled with sand,
Pretending to comb it with a big seashell hand.

Crashing waves have jokes, they tell in a roar,
"Did you hear the one about the sea-floor floor?"
A barnacle chuckles, another keeps score,
As the tide rolls in, with laughter galore.

Silence in the Salt

The tides speak softly, like a cheeky friend,
That nudges you gently, hoping you'll bend.
Seashells share secrets, all stacked in a line,
While snails in their homes just sip on their brine.

Gulls squawk about nothing, their humor a stretch,
"Why do fish swim? Because they can't go fetch!"
The crabs crack up over a clam's silly joke,
As a shrimp nearby turns, and whimsically pokes.

Mollusks relax, in their cozy shell caves,
Pondering life's mysteries with silly raves.
Anemones dance, having quite a bold feast,
While a flatfish just laughs, "I'm the oddest beast!"

All around the currents, laughter's the rule,
With bubbles of joy, it's the ocean's schooling tool.
Drifting with giggles, on waves fresh and free,
Who knew the ocean had such company?

The Breath of Nautical Shades

In the surf, there's a chuckle, like a tickle from foam,
Seahorses whisper of their daydreaming roam.
The fish wear their smiles, in mirthful parade,
While seaweed sways, in a wiggly charade.

Dolphins are jesters, with flips that delight,
They race with a laugh, through the soft moonlight.
Crustaceans burst out with sarcastic remarks,
As they shuffle along, leaving playful shark arcs.

Clownfish are clowns, with their colors all bright,
Making jest of the waves, in their watery flight.
A starfish observes with a grin on its face,
While a sea turtle glides with a leisurely grace.

The breeze joins in, whispering playful tunes,
Tickling the kelp as the sunset blooms.
In the deep of the ocean, where laughter prevails,
The tides swell with giggles, and joy never fails.

Dances of Hidden Currents

Currents twist secrets, like dancers on tiptoes,
Twisting and twirling, the ocean just glows.
Fish have their fun, in a swirling ballet,
While a barnacle grins, "I never move, hey!"

A group of sea urchins, giggling at plays,
Trade stories of crabs with their wiggly ways.
"Why cross the reef?" asks a wise old fish,
"To get to the kelp, that's my only wish!"

The waves clap their flippers in rhythmic delight,
As sea breezes whistle, under the pale light.
"Why are fish bad at playing cards?" they cry,
"Because they always peek when the others swim by!"

In the splash of the surf, shenanigans churn,
With every new moment, there's laughter to burn.
So dive into mirth, let your worries uncoil,
For the ocean's a stage, where humor can roil.

www.ingramcontent.com/pod-product-compliance
Lightning Source LLC
Chambersburg PA
CBHW070318120526
44590CB00017B/2723